VIOLENCE OUTSIDE THE TURKISH AMBASSADOR'S RESIDENCE: THE RIGHT TO PEACEFUL PROTEST

HEARING

BEFORE THE

SUBCOMMITTEE ON EUROPE, EURASIA, AND EMERGING THREATS

OF THE

COMMITTEE ON FOREIGN AFFAIRS
HOUSE OF REPRESENTATIVES

ONE HUNDRED FIFTEENTH CONGRESS

FIRST SESSION

MAY 25, 2017

Serial No. 115–36

Printed for the use of the Committee on Foreign Affairs

Available via the World Wide Web: http://www.foreignaffairs.house.gov/ or
http://www.gpo.gov/fdsys/

U.S. GOVERNMENT PUBLISHING OFFICE

25–558PDF   WASHINGTON : 2017

CONTENTS

VIOLENCE OUTSIDE THE TURKISH AMBASSADOR'S RESIDENCE: THE RIGHT TO PEACEFUL PROTEST

THURSDAY, MAY 25, 2017

House of Representatives,
Subcommittee on Europe, Eurasia, and Emerging Threats,
Committee on Foreign Affairs,
Washington, DC.

The subcommittee met, pursuant to notice, at 12:00 p.m., in room 2200 Rayburn House Office Building, Hon. Dana Rohrabacher (chairman of the subcommittee) presiding.

Mr. ROHRABACHER. I call this meeting of the Europe, Eurasia, and Emerging Threats Subcommittee to order.

Apologies to my colleagues for the short notice that we have given them but, due to the emergency nature of what has occurred, I believe strongly that we need to be heard on the record as soon as possible.

Nine days ago on May 16th, the President Turkey was visiting in Washington on a formal visit to the United States. It was during that trip that a group of American protesters that were concerned about the growing repression by the Erdogan regime in Turkey, gathered outside the residence of the Turkish Ambassador to exercise their right, as Americans, to have a peaceful assembly and to express their opinions.

Incredibly, security officers associated directly with the President, President Erdogan, his nominal body guards, broke past police lines and unashamedly attacked peaceful protesters in view of all the rest of us Americans.

The video of this ghoulish and fascistic attempt is appalling. At least 11 innocent Americans were bloodied and some of the Turkish security members were so brazen as to also scuffle with U.S. law enforcement personnel who were there trying to tone done the melee.

Furthermore, video evidence suggests that President Erdogan, himself, looked on as the attack took place. I find it hard to believe that well-trained security officials would watch such an explosive, unprovoked attack without the orders of their superior, especially knowing he was going to be there to witness it.

The attempt by members of the Turkish security service is an affront to the democratic values that we hold dear in the United States and was an act of supreme disrespect for the American people and our institutions.

This situation has only been made worse by the ongoing reaction by the Turkish Government, which summoned the U.S. Ambassador in Ankara, summoned to him to protest the actions of American law enforcement, as if it was aggressive.

Well, that, to have a president of a country, from another country, who watched his bully boys beat Americans into the ground and bloody them, and for him to protest our people, that is a supreme insult and I hope all Americans understand the message that he is giving us.

I will refrain from using a hand gesture of what he is giving us but we have a message for him: We don't need people like you visiting the United States anymore. You don't represent your people. When we want to talk to the Turks, we want to talk to Turks who want to have a democratic society and not to their oppressor and a man who is trying to create Islamofascism in his own country with him as the head fascist.

This arrogance is beyond the pale. Erdogan should never again be invited to the United States. He is an enemy of everything we stand for. More importantly, he's an enemy of his own people and we should side with the people of Turkey, not their oppressor. Perhaps such an incident would not be so offensive, except that it fits a pattern of broader political violence and suppression that has come to characterize the current Turkish Government, both at home and abroad.

I remind everyone that a similar incident occurred during President Erdogan's previous visit to Washington. Last March, while Erdogan spoke at a Brookings Foundation, his guards attacked protesters and journalists trying to cover the event. The repressive and authoritarian nature of the Erdogan Government has been developing and just basically becoming into being right in front of our eyes. A country that has been such a long friend of the United States, the people of Turkey who stood with us during the Cold War, when it was very risky to do so. And yes, the Soviet Union was pumping, at that time, millions of dollars into destabilized Turkey at that time but they stood with us. And now to have this leader, supposed leader, basically declaring that friendship is over and declaring that his people no longer have those democratic rights that they have enjoyed for these years, well, it is totally unacceptable.

And again, I am very proud that today we have a piece of legislation that is going through and will be quickly put before the body, as soon as we return in about a week.

So with that said, my friend, Mr. Cicilline, will be having his opening statement.

Mr. CICILLINE. Thank you, Mr. Chairman, for calling this meeting today and for giving us the chance to explore in detail what happened at the Turkish Ambassador's residence on May 16th, just a little over a week ago when President Erdogan's so-called security forces rudely assaulted peaceful protesters.

I want to thank our witnesses for being here today and to note that Ms. Usoyan, Mr. Yasa, and Mr. Hamparian were in attendance at the protest and will be sharing their firsthand accounts of what happened with us today. And I am glad that none of you were seriously injured in the incident on the 16th. And I thank all of you for being with us, as well as Professor Wedgwood for being here today to discuss this incident and how it will affect U.S.-Turkish relations going forward.

President Erdogan of Turkey recently consolidated his own control in a referendum giving him sweeping authority, as we all know, recently made an official visit to the United States to meet with President Trump. In that meeting, the two leaders discussed a variety of mutual interests, including the fight against ISIS, the failed coup plot against Erdogan last year, and other mutual interests.

I think it is important to note, to point out one thing that, by all accounts, was not discussed and that is Turkey's ongoing crackdown against fundamental freedoms, including freedom of the press and peaceful assembly. At no time did President Trump raise concerns about the crackdown being carried out by the Erdogan regime against dissidents, journalists, minorities, and anyone who speaks out against his government's abuses.

Later that same day, President Erdogan was leaving the Turkish Ambassador's residence when his guards became involved in an altercation with peaceful protesters, violently attacking Americans and others who were exercising their right to free speech on U.S. soil.

Multiple videos from the scene showed Turkish security forces beating, kicking, and otherwise assaulting protesters, with the DC Police officers attempting to break up the altercation. I understand we are going to see some of the video before this committee in just a few minutes. At least 11 individuals were seriously injured in the attack, with two requiring hospitalization.

Equally disturbing is the video that appears to show President Erdogan surveying the scene of protesters in front of him, then verbally encouraging his guards to attack. It is my understanding that two Turkish security officers were detained in relation to their involvement in this incident but were then released, due to diplomatic immunity. I also understand that there is still an active investigation into the incident by the Washington, DC Police Force.

Our State Department and Secretary Tillerson have rightfully condemned this egregious action by Turkish security forces and have called the Turkish Ambassador in to raise their concerns. These are good first steps but by no means do they resolve this issue.

There are a few steps that absolutely must be taken as followup to this horrific incident. The United States Government should request a waiver of immunity for anyone involved in the violent attack against peaceful protesters. The U.S. Government must make clear that we expect full cooperation by the Turkish Government into the investigation of this crime. The U.S. Government must make clear to Turkey and any other government who wishes to have a presence in the United States that our laws, including the freedom of speech and assembly are the binding laws of the land when they are on U.S. soil. And officials of the U.S. Government, including the President and Secretary of State Tillerson must make it clear that the protection of human rights and fundamental freedoms, including the right to free speech and freedom of assembly are American values and will be prioritized in our relationships with every country with whom we have relations.

To close, I want to emphasize that freedom, dignity, and equality are not just American values, they are universal values that every person deserves, no matter where they are born. This idea that we can somehow leave our values at our shore's edge to focus on other priorities is inherently false. Our values make us who we are; they guide how we live our lives and how we interact in the world.

The United States is a global leader precisely because people everywhere strive to achieve the freedoms that are afforded to us in our Constitution. When our top leaders say things such as we are not here to lecture or we don't expect others to adopt our values, it debases who we are, and the very ideals that form our democracy, and it has dire consequences.

I don't pretend that the Turkish Government has suddenly changed its tune because of the words of a few Government officials. They have been behaving badly on our soil for years. But this was a particularly brazen act on the heels of a highly publicized meeting with our President and one has to wonder why President Erdogan felt so emboldened that in the bright DC sunshine, in front of cameras and hundreds of people, he sent his attack dogs out.

As Secretary Tillerson said, this is simply unacceptable. Now, we must decide how we are going to respond as a country and as government representatives to this brazen assault on our people and our values. I think that the resolution that was passed by the full Foreign Affairs Committee this morning condemning this is an excellent start and I look forward to working with my colleagues to determine the appropriate reaction going forward.

And again, I thank the chairman for calling this meeting and I yield back.

Mr. ROHRABACHER. Thank you very much. And Mr. Brad Sherman for 5 minutes.

Mr. SHERMAN. Thank you.

This was not just an attack on American values, on international values of human rights, this was an attack on American sovereignty. Quasi-military forces of a foreign nation beat and attacked Americans on American soil. This was deliberate because Erdogan believes that this helps him politically back in Turkey. We have to demonstrate to the world that aggression on American soil is not going to pay off. We need to do more than just condemn what happened, not only recently but, as others have pointed out, at Brookings as well.

First, we have got to stop—we have got to emphasize that unless we get a formal apologize from Erdogan, himself, we will not even discuss with them their concerns about the YPG. We have already decided that these valuable allies in the fight against ISIS will get American arms. But the people of Turkey have to understand that we are not even willing to listen to a government that attacks Americans on American soil and brags about it, and boasts about it, and tries to benefit from it back in its own country.

The second thing we should do is prohibit the purchase or sale of the debt of the Turkish Government by Americans or American banks, and financial institutions, and exchanges, again, until we get a formal apology from Erdogan.

I realize such an apology might be politically difficult for him. That is the point. We have to illustrate this or we will have other leaders attacking Americans, both in their countries and in ours, for their own political reasons.

Why was Erdogan so emboldened? Because we have had an American Government that has cowered for generations, rather than recognize the Armenian genocide. If we are so weak that we are a party to genocide denial, who should respect our laws, or our sovereignty, or think that they will pay any price for anything they do here in our country?

Finally, the actions of those thugs have been compounded by the lies of the Turkish Ambassador. Keep in mind Erdogan was never in any danger whatsoever. The protesters were peaceful; they did not provoke any pro-Erdogan demonstrators. The statement of the Ambassador to the contrary is a lie on top of physical aggression and he should be asked to leave our country immediately.

So this is really a test for the United States. We know who Erdogan is. The question is: Who are we? Will we continue to be coward on the issue of the events of 1915 to 1923? Will we continue to walk on eggshells when we have a valuable ally in the fight against ISIS? And will we continue to see American banking institutions finance the Turkish Government at a time when Erdogan is able to extract political benefit from this attack on America?

We will see how we respond. The resolution we passed in committee today needs to be just the first step.

I yield back.

Mr. ROHRABACHER. Thank you, Mr. Sherman.

And I will introduce the witnesses now, and then we will show the video, and then we will return to the witnesses. I would hope that 5 minutes max—we all have to be out of here no later than two o'clock. So, we all need to watch the schedule on this. And again, I will introduce the witnesses, and then we will see the video, and then go to the testimony.

As witnesses today, we have three people and we have just been joined by a fourth who were present outside the Turkish Ambassador's residence on the 16th. Ms. Lucy Usoyan is a founder and president of the Ezidi Relief Fund, an organization which advocates for refugees and displaced persons in the region. She was severely beaten and, I understand, she is now, just now recovering.

Mr. Murat Yasa is a local small business owner and an organizer within the Kurdish community. He was involved in leading some of the protests that took place during President Erdogan's visit. He, too, received a pummeling by members of the Turkish Security Service for his efforts.

And Mr. Aram Hamparian, I hope I pronounced it correctly. Okay, he is the executive director of the Armenian National Committee of America, a political organization that represents the interests of Armenian-American community. He, too, was present for the attack on the 16th.

Finally, we have Ms. Ruth Wedgwood, a professor of international law and diplomacy at Johns Hopkins University School of Advanced International Studies. She has served on the U.S. Secretary of State's Advisory Committee on Private and Public International Law and she was a U.S. delegate to the U.N. Human Rights Committee and a member of the Pentagon Defense Policy Advisory Board, among many other things. She has earned her juris doctorate from Yale University and we are very, very grateful that on short notice she was able to join us.

Now with that, I think I would draw attention to my colleagues and to those who have come to the hearing today to the video which was compiled—how was this compiled? The people who were there, I believe this is from hand-held telephone cameras. Isn't it wonderful that we have that these days?

Aram, did you take the video?

Mr. HAMPARIAN. Some of it is from Voice of America and others from my cell phone.

Mr. ROHRABACHER. Okay, all I know is that I believe that the iPhone has done a lot to perfect our country by holding our law enforcement people accountable and also to protect our law enforcement people against unjust charges.

So with that said, here it is.

[Video shown.]

Mr. ROHRABACHER. Jesus. Look how courageous they are. Jesus. Is that it? Let me note that there was one video that I saw that wasn't included in this that had a picture of Erdogan, himself, observing this attack.

All of us should understand this is the United States of America. This is not Turkey.

This foreign leader, who treats his own people this way should understand that we are demanding an apology to these people, these Americans who were beaten here in the United States. And this is the way—if you think he is treating our people this way, how do you think he treats his own people? We know that. And he has taken a friendly country filled with people who like the United States and are friends of ours and turned them into prisoners and turned them into victims that we cannot ignore. We are on the side of a democratic Turkey and not this fascist, Islamic fascist dictatorship that Erdogan is superimposing on this people with that kind of violence.

Now, with that said, we will go to our witnesses. Again, we have got about 5 minutes a piece and 5 minutes for questions because we have got to be out of here at two o'clock. That gives us 1½ hours.

So, Ms. Lucy Usoyan, who I have already introduced.

STATEMENT OF MS. LUSIK USOYAN, FOUNDER AND PRESIDENT, EZIDI RELIEF FUND

Ms. USOYAN. Thank you so much. Well, with given opportunity I would like to first express my gratitude to Chairman Dana Rohrabacher, and Chairman Ed Royce, and all ranking members for sponsoring this hearing in such a short time frame.

As a citizen of United States of America, I feel very confident for my rights and I am honored to be here to testify on the peaceful protest attacked on May 16.

On May 16th, I was among those peaceful protesters by exercising my freedom of speech. I was expressing my personal opinion on President Erdogan's White House welcome event. I believe that individuals like Mr. Erdogan, who systematically abuse his authority by violating human rights, oppressing press, imprisoned second largest opposition party, both co-chairs and its members, committing war crimes, and strongly supporting ISIS terrorist group has no space in the White House of United States of America.

I am an Ezidi Kurd dissident by origin and my Ezidi people have suffered significantly in the aftermath of the ISIS attack on Sinjar District on August 2014. Moreover, March 2016 Erdogan's visit to Washington, DC, he had an event at Brookings Institute, where I and many Armenians, Syrians, Greeks, and Kurds had joined to a peaceful protest. As a result of Erdogan's angriness, he has contacted President of Azerbaijan, Aliyev, to attack Armenian Artsakh for 4 days.

In the aftermath of 4 days' attack, around 80 Armenian soldiers were killed and one was Ezidi origin soldier. He was beheaded by Ezidi soldiers and he happened to be my cousin.

So, I have many rights to express my angerness with Erdogan's abusive behavior. I was part of the peaceful protesters in the front of the White House. And once the event was over, me and others, we have walked toward Massachusetts Avenue to Turkish Ambassador's residency.

There was a large group of people in front of Turkish Ambassador's residency. As soon as we arrived, we began to hear cursings toward us and screamings at us. I could tell that the atmosphere became very tense, once the pro-Erdogan group saw us.

Police just asked to stay where we are and we stood and simply began our chantings, as we did in front of the White House. I could tell that we didn't have enough police officers right away. There was about five or so police officers but they were doing their best job.

And as we were chanting, I saw another group of about five people merging into existing group, pro-Erdogan's group, and running toward us. Those people were dressed differently. They were wearing dark sunglasses, and hacky t-shirts under unbuttoned shirts. They were wearing military boots, I think.

And I saw water bottles were thrown to us, one of which hit my leg and I felt hurt. It hurt as if something was burning my leg. And I saw cell phones flying around. It happened very quickly. I didn't have a chance to think, to run away, or to protect myself.

The next thing I know, I was on the ground and someone was kicking me in the head. I remember only one thought. I thought okay, I am on the ground; I don't even try to protect myself; what is the purpose of beating me? But then I lost unconscious.

When I opened my eyes I think it was over. I tried to get up but my legs were very heavy. I don't know why. I believe police officer helped me to get up or sit and I felt a massive headache and pain around my neck, and back, and head. I got shocked when I saw my friends' bloodied face.

That evening, I spent in George Washington Hospital, as well as all other injured, which were about eight or nine. The doctor gave me a pain killer and recommended to do a CAT scan to check my head condition but I refused because I don't have insurance yet.

The next morning, I opened my eyes and I feel extremely dizzy. I closed my eyes but it just got worse. And I tried to get up in my room but I just collapsed. And I am very thankful to my friends who came and visited me. They convinced me and they took me to the hospital. As a result, I end up in E.R. to the George Washington again and I was diagnosed with minor brain injury. The doctor says that I have bruises on my brain.

So, it will take me 6 weeks to recover. I think my time is over.

[The prepared statement of Ms. Usoyan follows:]

May 25, 2017

With given opportunity, I would like to, first express my gratitude to Chairman Dana Rohrabacher and Chairman Ed Royce and all Ranking members for sponsoring this hearing and making it happen in such a short time frame.

As citizen of United States of America, I fill very strong for my rights and I am honored to be here to testify on peaceful protest attack on May 16th 2017.

On May 16th, I was among those peaceful protesters, by exercising my freedom of speech, I was expressing my personal opinion on President Erdogan's White House welcome event.
I believe that the individuals like Mr. Erdogan who systematically abuses his authority, by violating human right, pressing press, imprisoning second largest party's co-chairs and its member's, committing war crimes, and strongly supporting a terrorist group like ISIS has no space in the White House of the United States of America.

I am Ezidi, Kurd dissident by origin, and my Ezidi people have suffered significantly in the aftermath of the ISIS attack on Sinjar district, on August 3rd, 2014.

Moreover, on March 2016 Erdogan's visit to Washington D.C. he had an event at Brookings Institute, where I and many Armenians, Assyrians, Greeks and Kurds have joined to a peaceful protest, as a result of Erdogan's angriness he has contacted to President Aliev of Azerbaijan, to attack Armenian Artsakh, the attack continued for 4 days. In the aftermath of the 4-day attack around 80 Armenian soldires were killed and one Ezidi origin solder was beheaded by Azeri solders, that solder happen to be my cousin… That said, I have many rights to express my angriness with Erdogan's abusive behavior.

I was a part on peaceful protestors in front of the White House and once the event was over. Me and others have walked towards Massachusetts Avenue, to Turkish Ambassador's Residency. There was a large group of people in front of the Turkish Ambassador's Residency. As soon as we arrived, we begin to hear cursing's and screaming's at us. I could tell that the atmosphere became very tense once pro-Erdogan's group saw us.

Police has just asked us to stay where we are, we stood and simply begun our chanting as we did in front of the White House. I can tell that we didn't have enough police officers right away, there was about 5 or 6 officers, but they were doing their best job.

As we were chanting, I saw another group, of about 5 people, merging into existing pro-Erdogan's group and running towards us. Those people were dressed differently, they were wearing dark sunglasses and hacky t-shirts under unbuttoned shirt, they were wearing, I think, military boots. And I saw-water bottles were thrown to us, one of which heat my leg and it hurt me as if something burned my leg, then I saw cell phones flying around.

It happened very quickly, I didn't have time to think to run away or to protect myself.
Next thing I know, I was on the ground and someone was kicking me in the head. I remember a thought, "Ok, I am on the ground, what's the purpose of beating me?" and then I lost unconscious.

When I opened my eyes, I think it was over. I tried to get up, but my lags were too heavy, I don't'
know why. I believe police officer has helped me to seat, and I felt a massive headache, and pain
in my back and my neck.
I got shocked when I saw my friend's faces covered with blood.

That evening I spent in the George Washington Hospital. The doctor gave me a pain killer and
recommend to do a cat scan to check my head condition, but I refused since I don't have insurance.
I got discharged.

Next morning when I opened my eyes, I felt extremely dizzy. I closed my eyes but it got only
worse. I tried to get up but I've lost my balance and collapsed.

I am thankful to my friends who came to visit me and have convinced to go back to the hospital.
As a result, I end up in ER again, this time they did a cat scan and diagnosed me with minor brain
injury, doctor explained that there are some little bruises on my brain, they discharged me and
have recommend to rest, and stated that it will take me up to 6 weeks to recover. I am still suffering
and I can't take total care of myself. Some days I feel good in the morning, and in the afternoon
I'm getting worse.

I don't feel save to be alone, and I don't feel save when I am in the city a lone. I have a feeling that
someone is following me or watching me. I don't know if I'll ever overcome all this problems, but
I've been thinking, it would've been better for me to never open my eyes. I am not use to, to not
feel confident about myself and to not be able to take care of myself.

Mr. ROHRABACHER. Thank you very much.
Mr. Yasa.

STATEMENT OF MR. MURAT YASA, LOCAL BUSINESSMAN AND PROTEST ORGANIZER

Mr. YASA. Good afternoon Chairman Rohrabacher and distinguished members of the subcommittee. Thank you for inviting me to testify today about the brutal attack on peaceful protesters, including myself, by Turkish security forces outside the Turkish Ambassador's residence on May 16, 2017.

I am proud father of U.S.-born children. My biggest accomplishment has been to provide my children the freedom and security that I was deprived of as a child in Turkey. So, imagine my disappointment and heartbreak when Erdogan and Turkish bodyguards violently attacked me for exercising my right to freedom of assembly on American soil.

As somebody that takes pride in the fundamental American values, it was hard for me to explain to my children why I was attacked and why Erdogan's goons were able to escape the U.S. without any justice.

For the past 30 years, I have attended countless protests because it is my right as an American citizen to do so. On Tuesday, May 16, 2017, I woke up early and I made my way into DC. I was there to protest against Erdogan as he visited the White House. I was there to protest against his direct attack on Kurds in Turkey. I was there to protest against unlawful imprisonment of Kurdish opposition. I was there to exercise my First Amendment Right. I was there as an American citizen.

Thereafter, a small number of us decided to continue our protest in front of the Turkish Ambassador's residence. We arrived there at approximately 2:45 p.m. There was 15 of us on the sidewalk across the Ambassador's residence. Among us were women and children under the age of seven. Just briefly after arriving, we began our protest and condemned Erdogan for his direct attack on the Kurds and the Kurdish children.

One of our slogans was dedicated to Mr. Selahattin Demirtas, who is the co-chair of the pro-Kurdish political opposition in Turkey. Mr. Demirtas has been unlawfully arrested and is still waiting for trial while in jail since November 2016.

Our posters were pictures of Mr. Demirtas. Our slogans were "freedom for Demirtas." Meanwhile, the pro-Erdogan supporters gathered across from us, across the street, were using insulting and vulgar words directed at us and children. After a verbal altercation, two pro-Erdogan supporters crossed the sidewalk and made their way into the street ready to attack us. The DC Police were able to intervene before the conflict escalated and attempted to get them back on the sidewalk.

Thereafter, the police remained in front of the Turkish protesters and tried to prevent them from attacking us. But after a few minutes, Erdogan's bodyguards, dressed in black suits and ties, pushed their way through the DC Police and attacked our group.

Erdogan's bodyguards were joined by the Turkish security personnel, as well as supporters. There was more than 50 of them, some armed, but all were ready to attack. They came at us with such a force that even the DC Police——

Well, let me get into the detail of the attacking. Whey they attacked, three, four of them, and I saw the lady, Ms. Usoyan, was next to me, one of them has grabbed her and started to punch her face and kicking. And I tried to cover her, tried to cover her head but I couldn't and I fell down. Four of them jumped on me. As you see on the picture, I am the one carrying the megaphone. And they kicked me one after another on my face. And I tried to get up but I couldn't and I realized that they are not going to let me get up and respond. So, I just tried to cover my head and I was unconscious. I don't know how long I was there.

When I get up, I saw it is bleeding all over and then the police officer, they have me.

My time is over.

[The prepared statement of Mr. Yasa follows:]

Murat Yasa Written Testimony
in front of the Subcommittee on Europe, Eurasia, and Emerging Threats

May 25, 2017

Introduction:

Good afternoon Mr. Chairman, Ranking Member Engel, and distinguished members of the Sub-committee. Thank you for inviting me to testify today about the brutal attack on peaceful protestors, including myself, by Turkish security forces outside the Turkish Ambassador's Residence on May 16, 2017.

I fled Turkey in the early 80's and came to the United States to pursue a better life. Indeed it was hard to leave my family behind, but it was worth for me because I firmly believed in the fundamental American values.

I am a proud father of U.S. born children. My biggest accomplishment has been to provide my children the freedom and security that I was deprived of as a child in Turkey. So imagine my disappointment and heartbreak when Erdogan and Turkish bodyguards violantely attacked me for exercising my right to freedom of assembly on American soil.

As somebody that takes pride in the fundamental American values, it was hard for me to explain to my children why I was attacked, and why Erdogan's goons were able to escape the U.S. without any justice.

To ensure justice is served is not for my benefit. It is for our children and the unpredictable future that lays ahead. To hold the perpetrators accountable for their unjustifiable and brutal attacks is not for my benefit. It is to reflect the values that is engraved in the hearts of all Americans.

For the past 30 years, I have attended countless protests, because it is my right as an American citizen to do so. On Tuesday, May 16, 2017, I woke up early and made my way into DC. I was there to protest against Erdogan as he visited the White House. I was there to protest against his direct attack on Kurds in Turkey. I was there to protest against the unlawful imprisonment of Kurdish opposition. I was there to exercise my 1st amendment right. I was there as an American citizen.

Thereafter, a small number of us decided to continue our protest in front of the Turkish Ambassador's residence. We arrived there at approximately 2:45 p.m. There was 15 of us on the sidewalk across the Ambassador's residence. Among us were women, and children under the age of 7. Just briefly after arriving, we began our protest and condemned Erdogan for his direct attack on Kurds and Kurdish children. One of our slogan was dedicated to Mr. Selahattin Demirtas, who is the co-chair of the pro-Kurdish political opposition in Turkey. Mr. Demirtas has been unlawfully arrested and still waiting trial while in jail since November 2016.

Figure 1 Our group on May 16, 2017, across the Turkish Ambassador's Residence

Our posters were pictures of Mr. Demirtas. Our slogans were "freedom for Demirtas." Meanwhile, the pro-Erdogan supporters, gathered across from us, across the street, were using insulting and vulgar words directed at us, and the children. After a verbal altercation, the pro-Erdogan supporters crossed the sidewalk, and made their way into the street, ready to attack us. The DC police were able to intervene before the conflict escalated, and attempted to get them back on the sidewalk.

Thereafter, the police remained in front of the Turkish protestors, and tried to prevent them from attacking us. But after a few minutes, Erdogan's bodyguards, dressed in black suits and ties, pushed their way through the DC police, and attacked our group. Erdogan's bodyguards were joined by the Turkish security personnel, as well as his supporters. There was more than 50 of them, some armed, but all were ready to attack. They came at us in such force, that even the DC police was unable to prevent them from charging at us. Although they tried, the DC police remained outnumbered and unable to protect any of us from the brutal attacks.

At any given time, there was at least five to six men over each one of the protestors. They repeatedly kicked us, threw punches, and left us with bloody heads and severe injuries.

As soon as I saw the men running towards our group, I turned around and saw one of the woman protestors, Lucy Osoyan, who is sitting next to me today. She was grabbed by two of the bodyguards, and being punched. I ran over to help her, but was kicked to the floor myself. Thereafter, more than 4 men brutally and repeatedly kicked me, as I laid on the cement floor. As I attempted to get up, I was kicked back to the ground each time. I remember closing my eyes, and all I could think about were my children.

I truly thought that I was going to die. I felt so helpless as I laid on the ground. And every time I thought that they were done attacking me, I would feel another kick to my face.

It was very hard for me to grasp what had just happened. It felt like a bad dream, but the pain was very real.

Thereafter, the kicks and punches finally came to a stop, and I was able to get myself up with the help of two DC police officers. My shirt was covered in blood, and my vision was blurry. I was in complete shock, and unable to observe what was going on around me. The DC police helped me sit on the grass, across from the place I was attacked. And as I sat there, I still could not believe the incident that unfolded just moments earlier.

The first ambulance to arrive, brought first-aid kits, and attempted to treat us at the scene. However, seven of us, including three women protestors, were later rushed to the emergency room at George Washington Hospital. Another woman protestor was sent to the Georgetown Hospital Emergency Room.

I was rushed into the ER upon arrival. My injuries included, a large cut on my nose that required stitches; bruised and swollen lip; one of my tooth was broken and three others became loose; and I had scratches across my face and my head. I was at the ER until 10:00 pm, and was sent home with pain medication. The doctors at the ER informed me that my swollen lip prevented them from accessing my teeth, and referred me to a specialist. I was also told to make an appointment with my primary physician, and follow-up about my severe injuries.

I was physically in pain, and emotionally drained. I could not comprehend what happened, and could not find the words to describe any of this to my family.

I arrived home late, and my wife and kids were waiting by the door. They greeted me with hugs, as they tried to fight back their tears. We went inside our home, and sat in our family room, with high emotions all around the room. I could not hide the tears from my wife or children. To see them again was what I kept envisioning as I was brutally beaten by the Turkish security forces. As I laid there bleeding, I did not think that I would get this opportunity, and so I held them a little tighter that night, and hugged them until they fell asleep.

It has been a little over a week since this brutal and violence incident. And I still cannot find a way to explain this to my children. How does a foreign government come to the United States and deprive us, American citizens, of the rights that the Constitution grants us? How could a brutal attack, such as this, happen on American soil? How can I explain to my children that the country we love, and the country we call home, is the place where I was stripped off my rights?

To let the aggressors and the perpetrators get away with the crimes committed against women, children, and myself, on American soil, is to set a dangerous precedent, with dangerous consequences.

I want to emphasize my gratitude to all of you here today. Thank you for your commitment to the fundamental American values, and our Constitution. Thank you for ensuring that justice is served, and that what Erdogan does to Kurds in Turkey, he cannot do to us in America.

In the following page, I have included few pictures of members of our group after the attack.

Me after being attacked by Turkish security forces

Woman protestor being head-locked by Turkish bodyguards

Protestor that was repeatedly kicked by Turkish bodyguards

Mr. ROHRABACHER. Thank you, very much.
Mr. Hamparian.

STATEMENT OF MR. ARAM HAMPARIAN, EXECUTIVE DIRECTOR, ARMENIAN NATIONAL COMMITTEE OF AMERICA

Mr. HAMPARIAN. Thank you, Chairman Rohrabacher, for your very powerful and principle leadership on this issue. Congressman Cicilline, and Congressman Sherman, thank you as well.

I have submitted a written statement and will touch on a few points in my spoken testimony.

Last Tuesday's attack was, at its heart, not just an attack against Americans but an attack on American values. The facts of the attack, as well as last year's assault at the Brookings Institute are well-known to the subcommittee, as is Turkish record of aggression at home and abuse as well.

As has been noted, I participated in the peaceful protest at Sheridan Circle and was a witness to the brutal assault. I was able to videotape much of it and share it with CNN, and the Associated Press, and others.

Rarely, if ever, has a foreign government's attack against peaceful protesters on American soil been so thoroughly documented or so well-reported. Thankfully, as the chairman noted, because of vital video and social media, President Erdogan, today, is finding he can't sweep this under the rug or explain it away with the help of his P.R. people, his apologists, or his well-paid lobbyists.

Having, by all accounts ordered this attack, he has gone on the offensive now, calling in our Ambassador and falsely accusing U.S. law enforcement of aggressive actions. What he ordered on the streets of our capital here in Washington, DC provides a small insight, but a very chilling insight, into the depth and the depravity of the violence visited every day upon citizens of Turkey out of our city and away from our cameras. Imagine how bad that is, if this is what they wanted to do in Washington, DC.

These are the facts. This is pretty much where we are. We are, I think, as Americans, at a moment of reckoning on this issue, not simply about Erdogan but ourselves. We know who Erdogan is. Now it is time for him to understand who we are.

This hearing, Mr. Chairman, is certainly about foreign policy. This is the Foreign Affairs Committee but, at a more fundamental level, it is about our shared American commitment to our First Amendment and our freedoms.

The question before us is how will we respond to Ankara exporting its intolerance and violence to our shores. How will we respond to Erdogan's unapologetic attempt to bully Americans as he has bullied his own citizens? How will we answer Erdogan's arrogance?

His attempts now, and these are disgraceful, to have us throw, have Americans throw our people, our police, and even our principles under the bus to avoid offending his irrational and hateful sensitivities is simply unacceptable. We cannot do that to the brave officers who sought to defend the protesters or the Americans who simply sought to give voice to their views.

The choice is ours. I would humbly and respectfully offer a couple of suggestions. One is that President Trump can break his silence on the issue and forcefully condemn this attack on peaceful protesters in our nation's capital.

Our Government, including our Department of Justice, should fully investigate and criminally prosecute the attackers, demanding that Turkey issue a blanket waiver of diplomatic immunity for all involved in this assault up and down the chain of command.

Last Tuesday, let's be clear, last Tuesday was a crime. It was not a conflict. Multiple felonies committed on film in plain sight of U.S. law enforcement.

The administration should, as Senator McCain and others have recommended, exercise our right to immediately expel Turkey's Ambassador from the U.S. This would represent both an expression of our national outrage but also a reaffirmation of our commitment to freedom of expression.

Legislatively, we look forward to the passage of H. Res. 354, which the committee favorably reported this morning and that has the support of the chairman and also the full committee chairman, Mr. Royce, and the bipartisanship of the House.

We also, and this speaks to what Congressman Sherman said, we should also encourage the adoption of H. Res. 220, a bipartisan measure seeking simply to apply the lessons of Turkey's genocide against the Armenians, the Greeks, the Assyrians, and other Christians, in order to prevent future atrocities.

Again, let's be very clear on this point. The same Recep Erdogan who attacks our people and disrespects our police is allowed to set U.S. policy on the Armenian genocide. This foreign dictator is the guy who green lights or stop lights whether or not Americans can speak out on a human rights issue and that is disgraceful.

He has been allowed, and this is disgraceful as well, President Erdogan has been allowed to revel, to revel in the spectacle of arm-twisting Americans into silence on a known case of genocide documented in our own archives. He has bullied us into silence on our history and now he has his values in our sites. It must stop and it must stop here.

In closing, let me thank you again, Chairman Rohrabacher, for your tremendous leadership on this issue. Let me also say that the public scrutiny is the best remedy for these types of things and, for that reason, this hearing is so very welcomed. Thank you, sir.

[The prepared statement of Mr. Hamparian follows:]

Aram Hamparian

Executive Director
Armenian National Committee of America

U.S. House of Representatives
Committee on Foreign Affairs
Subcommittee on Europe, Eurasia, and Emerging Threats

May 25, 2017

Violence Outside the Turkish Ambassador's Residence:
The Right to Peaceful Protest

Thank you Chairman Rohrabacher and Ranking Member Meeks for this opportunity to testify about the May 16th attack by Turkish President Erdogan's bodyguards against peaceful protesters outside the Turkish Ambassador's residence.

I participated in this peaceful protest at Sheridan Circle and was witness to this brutal assault on Americans and American values.

I personally saw unprovoked attacks by President Erdogan's bodyguards and others against civilians protesting the Turkish government's policies. The Turkish President's security detail was large, clearly well-trained, and extremely violent - kicking and punching protesters even after they had fallen to the ground defenseless and, in at least one case, unconscious. I did my best to help the injured and stayed with many of them later that evening while they were being cared for at the George Washington University Hospital's emergency room.

Live footage that I filmed for the Armenian National Committee of America Facebook page served as source video for CNN, the Associated Press, and other major media outlets. Our viral video spread news of this incident around the world and, along with excellent video and reporting by the Voice of America and others, helped place a global spotlight upon the Erdogan regime's increasingly violent efforts to suppress dissent, both at home and now, increasingly, abroad. Your leadership in educating your Congressional colleagues and the American public about this outrage is deeply appreciated.

At the time of the incident I felt certain that it was an orchestrated attack, launched on orders from above. Video evidence I have reviewed subsequent to the violence, including a frame-by-frame analysis by the Washington Post and an audio analysis by the Daily Caller, confirm my conviction that this attack was, in fact, launched at the direction of President Erdogan.

At the time, I offered live, on-the-scene comments. While rushed and shared in a stressful setting, my words then reflect my views today:

> "This is the very type of intolerance that has come to predominate in Turkey, and it is now been exported here. I was here. I saw every bit of this. I saw a group of peaceful protestors in Sheridan Circle - there is grassy area across the street from Turkish Ambassadors residence - they were protesting, exercising their Constitutional right to speak their mind, to hold signs, to share their opinion, to express their views."

> "They were rushed from across the street by a group of - a pro Erdogan crowd - broke through the police lines, attacked just literally anybody within reach, with their fists and anything else they could get a hold of, and they beat as many people as they could, they left many bloodied, many have been taken to the hospital. This is exactly the type of violence you see in Ankara and they're exporting it here. They're exporting it here. I'm going to repeat myself: It's one thing for the Turkish government to do that to its own citizens, and it's a terrible thing. It's another thing for us, as Americans, to see that exported to the United States, and it was exported to right here to the nation's capital. Right here, blocks from the White House!"

The fact that Erdogan would act in such a brazen and brutal manner against Americans during a high-profile visit to Washington, DC offers a chilling insight into the depths of violence his forces visit every day upon those in Turkey who - far from the media spotlight - dare to dissent against his despotic rule.

Last Tuesday's aggression by the Turkish government at Sheridan Circle is clearly part of an escalating and very troubling pattern. Having been allowed by U.S. Presidents - past and present - to enforce its gag-rule against honest U.S. remembrance of the Armenian Genocide, the Turkish government is now openly and unapologetically exporting its intolerance and violence to America.

Past incidents involving violence by President Erdogan's bodyguards include a 2011 attack on a United Nations security detail and also a March, 2016, assault on protesters and journalists outside the Brookings Institute here in Washington, DC. I took part in last year's Brookings protest and witnessed first-hand the violence visited by President Erdogan's security on people gathered, upon our internationally respected Embassy Row, to exercise their Constitutional rights.

President Erdogan is acting with remarkable arrogance and absolute disdain for our country, open disrespect for our police, and outright contempt for the principles that inspire and guide our democracy. The news that the Turkish Foreign Ministry has filed an official protest with U.S. Ambassador John Bass over the conduct of U.S. law enforcement offices is as outrageous as it is offensive.

By way of background, our protest in Sheridan Circle followed an early, larger demonstration held across the street from the White House in Lafayette Park. The ANCA co-hosted this protest, along with other civil society groups concerned about a broad array of Turkish violations of human rights, humanitarian standards, press freedoms, and international law.

Our Facebook event page was titled, "Protest Against The Erdogan Dictatorship," and invited supporters to "Join supporters of human rights, religious liberty, and regional peace at a rally outside the White House (in Lafayette Park) during President Trump's May 16th meeting with Turkish President Erdogan. Among the issues listed on this page were: Erdogan's post-coup consolidation of authoritarian power; mass arrests of the HDP leadership; vast purge of his political opposition; arrest of record numbers of journalists; restrictions on religious freedom and worship; Wikipedia ban and social media crackdown; aggression against Kurds in Syria and Iraq; anti-American rhetoric and actions; continued military occupation of Cyprus; obstruction of justice for genocide of Armenians, Assyrians/Chaldeans/Syriacs and Greeks, and; illegal economic blockade of Armenia.

Among those protesting alongside human rights advocates, Armenians, Kurds, Greeks, and others at Lafayette Park was a religious freedom group seeking Turkey's release of Pastor Andrew Brunson, a U.S. citizen from North Carolina who, after leading a Christian ministry in Izmir for more than two decades, has, since October of 2016, been unjustly imprisoned in Turkey on trumped up charges.

Mr. Chairman and Ranking Member, I very much appreciate the opportunity to share my testimony with you today and look forward to answering any questions.

———————

Mr. ROHRABACHER. That is why you wanted to have the Assyrian right away and let it sink into people's memory.
Mr. HAMPARIAN. Yes, sir.
Mr. ROHRABACHER. Ms. Wedgwood.

STATEMENT OF MS. RUTH WEDGWOOD, EDWARD B. BURLING PROFESSOR OF INTERNATIONAL LAW AND DIPLOMACY, SCHOOL OF ADVANCED INTERNATIONAL STUDIES, JOHNS HOPKINS UNIVERSITY

Ms. WEDGWOOD. Thank you very much, Mr. Chairman, for convening this enormously important and very timely hearing.

I used to be a prosecutor. I thought I was pretty tough, even when I was five-foot tall. And I was not particularly merciful to all of my defendants but I did think that I was doing something, not just in taking people off the street for its own sake, but deterring other people in engaging in like episodes. And I almost was killed, at one point, when the FALN bombed the Federal courthouse in 1982, when I was preparing my first RICO case. And my husband and I were there. We should have been goners but, happily, the bridge made of concrete quelled the blast.

So, I know what it is, indeed, and I deeply sympathize with my colleagues here who have felt that they were at the brink of death because it is a possible event for human beings.

As a prosecutor, certainly we did everything we could to try to quell terrorist groups with RICO and other measures. But I do think that to send the message now to Turkey, there does need to be fairly dramatic, demonstrative measures taken. Whether it hurts our tourist trade or not, I don't really care. I think this is a guy who is a thug; he's a gumba. He is not an ordinary human being. He has decided to be a bully. One could make the surmise that if he bullies individual people, he will tend to bully the region. Would he be a reliable ally? No. Does there have to be a change of leadership? Yes. I don't know how you do that. We have many modalities. We have sanctions. We have had other ways in the past.

The Turks have always been mistreated, I think, in Germany by not being allowed to naturalized. I have always been in favor of allowing them to naturalize in Germany but it is going to be much harder to make that argument if Turkey, itself, is so grotesquely mistreating people who fall into its power.

I know that it is complicated to quell ISIS and that there the kind of Game of Thrones that one has to play to keep alliances together is very, very tricky. But this kind of inconceivable, unabashed kvelling, if I may use a Yiddish word, kind of brutality will be copied by other countries around the world, too, if they see that it takes and it is effective.

So, if you want a China that is not particularly more outrageous than usual on human rights and civil liberties, then you have to do something about Erdogan. And that goes throughout the region; Duterte and the Philippines have become very difficult. There is a copycat effect in the moral politics of human rights.

So I would, indeed, endorse what the chairman has done of treating this with the utmost sobriety and making it plain to President

Donald Trump that he can't be best buds with this guy; no skiing, no bowling, no hugs, rather, I would PNG him.

Thank you.

[The prepared statement of Ms. Wedgwood follows:]

Statement of Ruth Wedgwood
Edward B. Burling Professor of International Law
Johns Hopkins School of Advanced International Studies
Former U.S. member, United Nations Human Rights Committee
1619 Massachusetts Avenue, NW
Washington, D.C. 20036

Before the Committee on International Affairs
Subcommittee on Europe, Eurasia and Emerging Threats
U.S. House of Representatives
Dana Rohrabacher (R-CA) Chairman

Violence Outside the Turkish Ambassador's Residence and the Right to Peaceful Protest

Mr. Chairman and Members of the Subcommittee:

Freedom of speech and freedom of assembly are among the most precious rights that belong to American citizens and to our neighbors from abroad who have taken up residence in our beloved country.

The right to speak freely -- and to bear witness by assembling in public -- are prerogatives that have allowed the United States to make its own moral progress on issues such as civil rights and equality.

As Americans, we like to think that these rights are universal, and that they should not be subject to evasion or avoidance by foreign governments that disrespect their own people.

Indeed, in 1948, both the United States of America and Turkey voted in the U.N. General Assembly to adopt the historic Universal Declaration of Human Rights, guaranteeing the "right to freedom of peaceful assembly and association" (UDHR article 20) and the"right to freedom of opinion and expression" (UDHR article 19).

Yet last week, on May 16, there was a dreadful episode of violence in which protesters assembled at Sheridan Circle, in front of the residence of the Turkish ambassador, were subjected to gratuitous and outrageous beatings by persons who were apparently part of the security detail of President Erdogan.

There is no excuse for this. Any security concerns on the part of the Turkish delegation could have been handled by notifying the Metropolitan Police Department and seeking their assistance. Instead, the videotape seems to indicate that members of the Turkish security detail, dressed in plain clothes, left the ambassador's residence and crossed the street to assault demonstrators on the roundabout of Sheridan Circle, including by throwing metallic objects and beating them with sticks.

This is completely unacceptable on any occasion, but particularly during a state visit in which two countries are supposed to discuss serious issues. It is eerie, in the extreme, to see a photograph of President Erdogen peering out the window at the continuing violence, with no apparent attempt to stop the outrage.

These dastardly events are even more eerie and loathesome in light of the location of the attack. It was 41 years ago, on September 21, 1976, in the same area of Sheridan Circle, that a car bomb was exploded by Chilean agents seeking to assassinate political dissident Orlando Lettelier and his associate Ronni Moffet. Both Lettelier and Moffet were killed.

I am an admirer of the longer ambitions of Turkey, with Ataturk's creation of a secular state and adoption of modern methods of education and governance. There have been times when critics could object to how some other countries in Europe, including Germany, were reluctant to allow resident Turks to become citizens. Turkey has been an important partner of the United States in strategic matters, including fighting terrorism. Istanbul is a destination of choice for thousands of American tourists, and is a popular place to change planes on longer journeys to Asia.

But this "state visit" was a disaster, and must be acknowledged as such by the government of Turkey. The deliberate fomenting of violence and chaos was wholly inappropriate – and was in fact gravely shocking – for any serious political leader. It will scare off the very tourists that one might wish to attract to see the wonders of Turkey's Hagia Sophia and Topkapi Palace. And it is a blow against Turkish-Americans and the Turkish people.

As a former U.S. member of the United Nations Human Rights Committee, sitting in Geneva and New York over the course of eight years, as a former vice chair of the NGO known as "Freedom House", as a former federal prosecutor, and as an American citizen, I must decry this breach of the peace and the injuries caused to innocent civilians by this maladroit and unnecessary episode. U.S.-Turkish relations are too important to be eroded by stupidity like this.

Mr. ROHRABACHER. Thank you very much.

Mr. POE. Tell us what you really think.

Mr. ROHRABACHER. We will have Mr. Cicilline and then I will recognize Judge Poe, who has just joined us, and then Mr. Sherman, and I will do the wrap-up. And I would ask for 5 minutes each, if I can.

Mr. CICILLINE. Thank you, again to our witnesses and I am very sorry that you had the experience that you had and seeing it on the video makes it even more disturbing.

I think it is worth noting again that the response given by the Turkish Embassy was not only inaccurate, it was horrifying because it attempted to blame you, the victims, and others for the conduct of these security forces. And so it compounds the offense to this country and to citizens of America.

I want to first just ask the witnesses who were there and observed this, did any of you actually seen President Erdogan, either before, during, or after the attack? Did anyone actually see him?

Mr. YASA. The position we were, we would never be able to see him.

Mr. CICILLINE. You wouldn't have been able to see him, okay.

Mr. YASA. But we realized that when he arrived, there was a noise came from his supporters and we understood he was there.

Mr. CICILLINE. And were able to see, any of you, where the attackers, the men in the dark suits, went after the attack?

Ms. USOYAN. Where did they go?

Mr. CICILLINE [continuing]. They go after the attack?

Ms. USOYAN. They came to attack us.

Mr. CICILLINE. Right and then after it was over, did you see where they went?

Ms. USOYAN. They went back to the Turkish Ambassador's residency.

Mr. CICILLINE. Okay.

Ms. USOYAN. Actually, they were in a very harsh conflict with DC Police officers.

Mr. CICILLINE. And you actually saw them go back into the residence of the Turkish Ambassador?

Ms. USOYAN. Yes because I was asking police officers why do you guys don't arrest these people; you eye-witnessed this. And one police officer has asked me to identify some of them who I really remember and I identified some of them. But while I was identifying I could hear them screaming at some other police officers, yelling at them, saying you guys can't do your job and not competent.

Mr. CICILLINE. And that day or subsequent to that day, have each of you been in contact or have been interviewed by the DC Police Department?

Ms. USOYAN. Yes, I have.

Mr. YASA. Yes.

Mr. HAMPARIAN. Yes, and we have provided evidence to the Secret Service and the DC Police.

Mr. CICILLINE. I do think that it is important to make mention that, as we think about the veracity of statements coming out of the Turkish Embassy, we must be reminded of the refusal of the Turkish Government to acknowledge the Armenian genocide. It calls into question not only their treatment of the three witnesses we have heard from but their willingness to accept the truth and to share that and so it should maybe not be surprising but it is still disappointing to see the statement that the Turkish Ambassador issued. And I appreciate you coming before this committee today and sharing your firsthand accounts of what is a deplorable incident and something that we have responsibility to address in a very, very serious way.

Professor Wedgwood, my first question really is can you help us understand what legal recourse we have against the Turkish guards who were involved in this attack? Will all of them be protected by diplomatic immunity and is there a mechanism for Turkey to waive that immunity, if they wanted to?

Ms. WEDGWOOD. If Turkey wants to offer the conceit, the fiction that this was not authorized from the top, then they would waive the immunity. They would say these were guys out on a holiday; they were having some fun; they got carried away; and, therefore, we waive their immunity. That would discourage other people in the security services from ever taking that role again, by the way.

Mr. CICILLINE. So, in other words, if the actions that these guards took was not authorized by the President of the country or its official, then they do not enjoy diplomatic immunity?

Ms. WEDGWOOD. First, the lower down the food chain you get, the less immunity you have. So, permanent representatives at the U.N. or ambassadors get absolute full-tilt immunity. As you go down the rank order of the ordinary structure of an embassy, you get to official acts immunity pretty quickly. So a cook or a driver, at best, would have official acts immunity.

One can make the argument none of this was official acts. Official acts are where you go across the street and you accidently stumble and hit a woman on your way vote at the General Assembly. But deliberate malicious attacks like this, these are not official acts.

Mr. CICILLINE. So doesn't that argue for charging these offices and letting them claim and prove that they are entitled to diplomatic immunity?

Ms. WEDGWOOD. I might be inclined to have a little—I don't mean this in the way it is going to sound—fun just to take what happens to an ordinary perp when he's arrested.

Mr. CICILLINE. Right.

Ms. WEDGWOOD. And then we can have a debate in court and it will go up to the Supremes on whether or not they are immune. But that, itself, is a very important kind of political—I don't use the word theater advisedly but it is an expose of the vulgarity of what they did.

Mr. CICILLINE. Thank you very much. I yield back.

Mr. ROHRABACHER. We are now joined by distinguished jurist but also a great member of the United States Congress from Texas, Judge Poe.

Mr. POE. I thank the chairman and thank all of you all for being here. All of you all is plural to y'all, in case you were wondering. Being from Texas, I just wanted to tell you our language.

This episode that occurred against you three and the other protesters just makes me so mad that this would occur in the United States. How ironic it is that you are out there protesting and demonstrating for basic civil rights in Turkey and Erdogan and his Gestapo gang come over here and try to prevent you from having basic civil rights in the United States. I find that appalling.

I mean I am a former judge. Don't hold that against me. But you know a constitution is a big deal. We are unique among nations because we have this concept of the Bill of Rights. And the First Amendment is first because it is the most important amendment. And the right to free speech and peaceably assemble are both in the First Amendment, two of the five. And I am convinced they are there because that First Amendment is the most important. If you don't have that one, you don't have the rest of them.

And so I find this very disturbing. What I saw on the video is what most people did see, that all of a sudden, here comes this gang of folks and start beating up people who are just exercising the First Amendment in the United States.

And I find it reprehensible that a tyrant from another country would come to the United States and violate our basic Constitution so flagrantly. And I saw him in the video and he is looking at what is taking place. And then he casually goes on into the embassy for supper or whatever they were doing.

So, it seems to me that there needs to be some consequences. And on the diplomatic level, I am not sure what they ought to be. I have been called a lot of things but I have never been called diplomat. And I find this something that we just have to deal with—foreign power in the United States violating the First Amendment of the Constitution. That is a big deal when that happens and you can prosecute all the cases, as far as I am concerned. Ms. Wedgwood, you'd be glad to do that.

Do any of you believe or know that the attack was ordered by Erdogan or was it made by a decision of the security folks. Do any of you know that? Does anyone want to answer that?

Mr. HAMPARIAN. I can tell you at the time I felt, I was convinced that an order was given and the guys attacked because it felt like that. There was a tension in the air and then someone pulled a trigger and the attack started. But that is all I knew. It was just a feeling from the other side of the street.

And then when I watched the video of President Erdogan's guards and some journalists did like a frame-by-frame analysis, and they did some audio analysis where they pulled—played with the audio in order to be able to hear exactly what was being said, and that confirmed in my mind my hunch that this was ordered.

And it seemed very much, from the video, that the word came from the car, where President Erdogan was sitting, to his advisor, to a bodyguard, and then boom, all within 5 seconds.

Mr. YASA. In Turkish, he says [speaking foreign language.] means this is what he says. He says, attack, attack in that video.

So, we have no doubt that the order comes directly from Erdogan.

Ms. WEDGWOOD. And at a minimum, he could have turned it off right away and he didn't.

Mr. POE. Well, that is what I was saying. He is standing there watching it. Rather than say stop, he goes into the embassy or the Ambassador's house, like just utter contempt for protesters.

Are the three of you all going back out there and protesting some more in front of the Turkish Embassy?

Mr. HAMPARIAN. Judge, if you are there, we have your back. We will be there any day, any time, night or day.

Mr. CICILLINE. He already offered in the Foreign Affairs Committee to go jointly.

Mr. POE. We got a lot of yays in the Foreign Affairs Committee to go back out there with you and protest, mainly protesting the denial of free speech.

Mr. HAMPARIAN. I think simply the presence of Members of Congress in that circle at any time, at a time that works for the Members, even if it is a short visit, it would be so powerful and so symbolic. Offer some remarks and, basically, remind the Turkish Government that that soil is American soil.

I felt very strongly—this is a hunch I had, again on the day of— was the people who did the attacking felt like this was their world. There was no hesitance, no reticence whatsoever. There were police telling them to stop and they ignored it the way I have never seen anyone ignore the police on American soil. It was total arrogance; this is our place. And let's remind them, that is not their place. Sheridan Circle is ours, it is American.

Ms. WEDGWOOD. And if I could just add, Congressman, that is a diplomatic neighborhood, the American Society of International Law, which has a townhouse, which they finally paid off, is about 15 degrees around the circle and there are lots of other diplomatic establishments there. So, this is like the schmatta district for diplomats.

Mr. POE. Well, as far as I know, this has never happened in the United States by any other embassy that has been here or any other ambassador or head of state.

Once again, I find this appalling.

I thank you for the extra time, Mr. Chairman. I yield back to you.

Mr. ROHRABACHER. All right, so the word is out to the Erdogan Gang; Judge Poe is on the way and he is taking the posse. He's bringing a posse with him, including me.

Mr. YASA. Can I say something?

Mr. ROHRABACHER. Yes, sir, and then Mr. Sherman.

Mr. YASA. Oh, I am sorry.

Mr. ROHRABACHER. Go ahead and say it.

Mr. YASA. Well, I am definitely going to go protest Erdogan in front of the Turkish Embassy but this time I am not only carrying the megaphone, I want to make sure I have a baseball bat, too.

Mr. ROHRABACHER. Mr. Brad Sherman.

Mr. SHERMAN. Yes, before I focus on the events of the embassy, Ms. Usoyan, the Ezidi people are among the or probably the most oppressed people from ISIS. Which countries and groups in the area have provided safe haven or otherwise cooperated in the protection of the Ezidis?

Ms. USOYAN. Well there have been a lot of countries that accept Ezidi refugees.

Mr. SHERMAN. I mean in the area. I know that do.

Ms. USOYAN. So, as you know, I have traveled to the region and I saw very protected Ezidis in Northern Syrian, which is under control of YPG currently, because their rights as Ezidi minority have been respected. They have not been placed in the camps with Muslim refugees or even Christians. They have separate camp and they were very thankful for what they have.

Mr. SHERMAN. So the YPG has been helpful. Any other groups that have protected the Ezidis there?

Ms. USOYAN. Yes, in the attack, in the August attack it was YPG who created Green Corridor and about 50,000 Ezidis, they flee to Northern Syria.

As of today, I visited the camp which is hosting 5,000 families.

Mr. SHERMAN. And how has the Turkish Government treated the Ezidis?

Ms. USOYAN. Well, there was a case last year that Ezidis were trying to travel to Hungary and they were beaten up and placed in the prison. Yes, and now there was only a few camps that was under districts or control of HDP. So, that right has been taken away from HDP and Ezidi refugees has been spread all over the Turkey. So, it is very, very difficult for Ezidis for to survive in Turkey.

Mr. SHERMAN. I want to now focus on a reaction to this Turkish outrage. Erdogan lives by fanning grievance mentality in Turkey. And I don't want to help him do that. At the same time, we need to respond.

We have got Mr. Gulen living in the United States. The Turkish Government has made a number of claims for his extradition. I think we have to declare very firmly they have got no credibility. There is nothing that makes me feel better about Mr. Gulen than the attacks that come from Ankara. I mean I was suspicious of the guy until I heard the attacks from Ankara.

There is no credibility in the charges and certainly no credibility that if he were ever to be in Turkey that he would be treated with justice.

We can expand our involvement with the YPG. We have already decided to do that, now that Mr. Flynn is no longer making these decisions or helping to shape them.

We haven't talked about forcing them to waive civil liability but those who suffered should be able to sue the Turkish Government. There is more than ample evidence. And perhaps that being an economic matter, we can tie it, as I said before, to allowing Turkish debt to be sold in the United States or purchased by Americans.

We have already talked about expelling their ambassador. Obviously, our failure to recognize the genocide emboldens Erdogan every day.

From amongst this pallet of possible reactions or others, I would like our witnesses to say what do we do that demonstrates to the Turkish people that this kind of thuggery is harmful to their interests? What do we do to punish and seek recompense from the Erdogan Government without playing into his grievance game?

Ms. USOYAN. If I may, I really have a good list of proposals and I think you will just smile and you would agree with me but I just want to make sure that this hearing has a follow-up and Turkish Government will proceed to see the consequences from U.S. authorities. Because if next time, let's say, President Erdogan, he comes, I will make sure to go to the front line and begin to chant whatever I was chanting on Tuesday, May 16th but I am just afraid that if we let this go unnoticed or unfollowed, they will just kill us next time.

And social media has covered it worldwide and I receive messages from all around the world. It doesn't show our leadership as strong if such action is happening.

Mr. SHERMAN. Do we have anything to add, keeping mind that persuading the Trump administration to do anything, I mean we got a statement out of Tillerson, has been difficult. Some of these things could be done by Congress.

So, Mr. Hamparian.

Mr. HAMPARIAN. It is in the President's hands but the expulsion of the ambassador I think would send a good message. That is the language of diplomacy. And also, Ambassador Kilic is a partisan to this issue. He is not, in my opinion, sort of career foreign service guy. He's a Erdogan guy. He was out there yelling at the cops. That is the right message and I think it would be the right one to send.

Mr. SHERMAN. And Congress could, of course, pass a resolution calling upon him to be expelled and, perhaps going further, in declaring that Members of Congress shouldn't meet with him.

And Ms. Wedgwood, if you have——

Ms. WEDGWOOD. Oh, I am trying to be creative. He doesn't necessarily need the big residence that he has. If somebody is here, ordinarily, one respects the suggestion of the Government as to what grand house on Massachusetts Avenue they might choose to inhabit but it doesn't—and I suppose the property is—it would be interesting to look at the title to the property and see who owns it.

But certainly, in his ambassadorial function, that can be taken away, or one can demand that it could be for a much smaller, darker——

Mr. SHERMAN. I am worried about the tit for tat and I am especially worried about the safety our diplomats in Ankara.

Ms. WEDGWOOD. That is true.

Mr. SHERMAN. Any other comment? I have gone over. I yield back.

Mr. ROHRABACHER. Thank you very much, Mr. Sherman.

I remember years ago there was a movie about guys in black. Do you remember that movie? It was the Men in Black. The Men in Black and I am looking at these guys running across the way in their black outfits. I mean this is right out of a sick B movie. The Men in Black, they were out to expose monsters. In this movie, the men in black are the monsters and they are working for the monster who is watching on the side.

Brad, you made a good point about Gulen, about we remember this, the perception that we now have of the Turkish Government and of Erdogan, himself, has now been shaped and changed forever. He will never—he can come and beg forgiveness all he wants. We have his number now.

The American people, we have tried our best to reach out to Turkey, trying to give every benefit of the doubt. I had four hearings on Turkey trying to make sure, in each one of them, trying to make sure that they knew exactly how we appreciated the friendship of the Turkish people, especially during the Cold War. And what this

has done now is exposed us to the fact that they have an oppres-
sive government there that is totally different than those people
who worked with us during the Cold War.

They are no longer our friends because the President, the head
of their country now, can watch this and then call our ambassador
in to castigate us, after seeing this firsthand. He saw this firsthand.

One wonders then, when he talks about Gulen, we have to take
into consideration what he did here. Obviously, you have a fascist
megalomaniac in charge of the Government of Turkey who is so
consumed with his own power that he thinks that he can call people together and tell us that we are wrong, when we see our citizens being beaten into the dirt, American dirt.

So, we must take that into consideration when he—this is the
guy he wants to close down all these schools. The Gulen movement—after this, we should note the Gulen movement is probably
a very positive thing. Those of us who are kind of okay, what is
this all about, well this should cement what we think of them.

We also needed to know what we thought about the supposed
coup that took place in which Erdogan, himself, assumed so much
power using the supposed coup as an excuse. If Erdogan can sit
and watch this and then ask us for an apology, what does that tell
us about his honesty in dealing with his own people? I would say
that if there was ever any doubt that that was a phony coup, that
Erdogan has used in order to destroy his opposition or anyone who
disagrees with him in Turkey, this should settle those issues as to
whether or not he is a megalomania fascist or whether not he is
just a president who is in a volatile situation.

I would ask my colleagues to, again, join me in working with
Judge Poe. If this man tries to come, I have pledged today at the
hearing that I would be of Judge Poe outside that embassy.

Now, a couple last thoughts. And that is, look, this is not the
first time this has happened in America. Okay? There have been
other cases where dissidents have been here and they have been
beaten up. The Chinese I know, about 10 years ago, we saw this
happen with some Chinese—in fact it might have been 20 years
ago now, when you had Chinese people demonstrating and they
ended up being beaten up by people coming from out of their embassy. That doesn't happen anymore. We put a stop to that.

But you know this isn't something that we can—as we have said
here today, this will determine who we are. After all these words,
what I just said what Erdogan is, what we do now will determine
who we are. That will determine also what kind of President we
have.

I will have to say that I am a little disturbed. And of course, I
am one person who tries to put things in perspective. I would say
this is, if the State Department can deal with this when they are
so tough on what the Russians, whenever the Russians get out of
line, and I voted with you today in condemning the Russians who
got out of line, that tells us something. We need to make sure that
things are in perspective and Erdogan has now defined for us that
perspective. We expect that, as Americans, we will make sure that
he understands that he is the one who set the rules. He's the one
who has established the perception and the type of relationship we

will have and it is not going to be like it was 10 years ago with a friendly Turkish Government, where we tried to give them the benefit of the doubt every time we could. That will not happen again.

So with that said, I am going to give each one of my fellow members 1 minute to end and then I am going to give you guys the last say for 1 minute.

Brad, you have got 1 minute.

Mr. SHERMAN. I think it has been said. This is a test of who we are and how we react. And I look forward to working with members of the subcommittee to do more than token responses, until such time as Erdogan formally and personally apologizes for what happens.

Mr. CICILLINE. Thank you again, Mr. Chairman. You know when we speak about foreign policy, we typically speak about the best interests of the American people and the national security interests of the United States. We don't typically contemplate, in the discussion of foreign policy, that it implicates the protections of the American people on our own soil from violent actions of a foreign government.

But I think the chairman is right. This is a moment in which the commitment of the United States, in terms of our basic human rights, our basic freedoms, that we are so proud of, that we hold up to the world, our commitment to that will be tested by the way that we respond to the actions of a foreign government coming to America and attacking people who are peacefully protesting, which is a bedrock of our democracy. And I promise, as a member of this subcommittee, and as a Member of Congress, I will do all that I can do to vindicate those sacred rights and insist that the Turkish Government, that President Erdogan accept full responsibility for his conduct and that we stand strong in the view of the rest of the world with respect to our commitment to important human rights.

And with that, I yield back.

Mr. ROHRABACHER. Judge Poe.

Mr. POE. Thank you, Mr. Chairman. I think our message should be to the tyrant that you don't mess with American citizens and their constitutional rights or you will rue the day that you ever did.

Now, let us make sure there is a consequence for what occurred against you.

I yield back to you, Mr. Chairman.

Mr. ROHRABACHER. And I will yield 1 minute to each of our witnesses to sum up. One minute, then we have got to go.

Ms. USOYAN. Well, I have always been proud to be citizen of America, of United States of America. Now, seeing a great response from Congress, from Senate, from fellow Americans, I feel so thankful and so grateful for the fact that I am on this land, and that my rights are protected, and I have people who care deeply about me. I feel very much loved and I really appreciate all of your work.

Mr. YASA. Thank you so much. It is my honor to be here in front of you. And it is my also honor to be American citizen. And the best thing I gave my children, they were born here and they are American citizens that is the best thing that happened to them.

And last sentence, as a Kurd from Turkey and American citizen, if this is what they do to us here, imagine what they do, the Kurds, Armenian, Greek, others against the Government in Turkey, what they do.

Mr. ROHRABACHER. Excellent point. Thank you.

Mr. HAMPARIAN. I would just offer that probably within minutes of this video going viral, the Turkish lobby kind of like started racking up their billable hours and they are going to work the State, they are going to work The Hill, they are going to work the White House, they are going to do all that stuff to try to manage this process, and dumb it down, and get us past it, and cover it up, and explain it away.

So I would simply say I encourage the subcommittee, respectfully encourage the subcommittee to follow-up with DOJ and to follow up with the DC Police just to make sure that these prosecutions move forward. There were multiple felonies committed on film. Some of them were diplomatic and some are out of the country. Others are here and the prosecution should move forward. If they don't move forward, that will be the barometer. That will be the canary in the coal mine that this is getting massaged and covered up.

Ms. WEDGWOOD. I would do two things. One is I would have one of you gentlemen or all five of you—four of you—five of you to have a mano a mano with President Trump and make clear to him, in private, why he ought not to cozy up to this guy because I am not sure that there has been enough distance from the White House, vis-a-vis Erdogan. And it is just bad mojo all the way around, if the White House appears to be congenial.

I also would be curious where Erdogan keeps his money. Everybody has offshore accounts, Channel Islands. You name it, they have got it. And while I am sure he has his fortunes scattered around the world, it would be interesting to know and it is not that hard to find out nowadays where folks have their money. And if there are people who have suffered damages as a consequence, when and if he leaves office, or if some country chooses to take a narrow interpretation of Presidential immunity, there are suits to be filed and fun to be had.

Mr. ROHRABACHER. Thank you. I want to thank all the witnesses on behalf of these United States. U.S., it is just us. That is all it is, the United States, every race, every religion, and every ethnic group made up in this family of Americans. And we will determine what we are outraged by and act upon what our values really are not just what our words are. If he attacks one American, he attacks all.

This hearing is adjourned.

[Whereupon, at 1:19 p.m., the subcommittee was adjourned.]

APPENDIX

Material Submitted for the Record

SUBCOMMITTEE HEARING NOTICE
COMMITTEE ON FOREIGN AFFAIRS
U.S. HOUSE OF REPRESENTATIVES
WASHINGTON, DC 20515-6128

Subcommittee on Europe, Eurasia, and Emerging Threats
Dana Rohrabacher (R-CA), Chairman

May 24, 2017

TO: MEMBERS OF THE COMMITTEE ON FOREIGN AFFAIRS

You are respectfully requested to attend an OPEN hearing of the Committee on Foreign Affairs, to be held by the Subcommittee on Europe, Eurasia, and Emerging Threats in Room 2200 of the Rayburn House Office Building (and available live on the Committee website at http://www.ForeignAffairs.house.gov):

DATE: Thursday, May 25, 2017

TIME: 12:00 p.m.

SUBJECT: Violence Outside the Turkish Ambassador's Residence: The Right to Peaceful Protest

WITNESSES: Ms. Lusik Usoyan
                       Founder and President
                       Ezidi Relief Fund

                       Mr. Murat Yasa
                       Local Businessman and Protest Organizer

                       Mr. Aram Hamparian
                       Executive Director
                       Armenian National Committee of America

                       Ms. Ruth Wedgewood
                       Edward B. Burling Professor of International Law and Diplomacy
                       International Law and Organizations Program
                       School of Advanced International Studies
                       Johns Hopkins University

By Direction of the Chairman

37

COMMITTEE ON FOREIGN AFFAIRS

MINUTES OF SUBCOMMITTEE ON _______ *Europe, Eurasia, and Emerging Threats* _______ HEARING

Day___ *Thursday* ___Date____ *May 25, 2017* ___Room___ *Rayburn 2200* ___

Starting Time ___ *12:00 p.m.* ___ Ending Time ___ *1:19 p.m.* ___

Recesses |__*0*__| (___to ___)(___to ___)(___to ___)(___to ___)(___to ___)(___to ___)

Presiding Member(s)

Rep. Dana Rohrabacher

Check all of the following that apply:

Open Session ☑   Electronically Recorded (taped) ☑
Executive (closed) Session ☐   Stenographic Record ☑
Televised ☐

TITLE OF HEARING:

Violence Outside the Turkish Ambassador's Residence: The Right to Peaceful Protest

SUBCOMMITTEE MEMBERS PRESENT:

Rep. Cicilline, Rep. Poe, Rep. Sherman

NON-SUBCOMMITTEE MEMBERS PRESENT: *(Mark with an * if they are not members of full committee.)*

N/A

HEARING WITNESSES: Same as meeting notice attached? Yes ☑ No ☐
(If "no", please list below and include title, agency, department, or organization.)

STATEMENTS FOR THE RECORD: *(List any statements submitted for the record.)*

Attached

TIME SCHEDULED TO RECONVENE _______
or
TIME ADJOURNED ___ *1:19 p.m.* ___

Subcommittee Staff Associate

Statement for the Record
Submitted by Mr. Connolly of Virginia

As a co-chair of the Congressional Caucus on U.S.-Turkey Relations and Turkish Americans, I am a firm supporter of the U.S.-Turkey alliance. Turkey is a NATO ally and an important partner in the fight against ISIS. Turkey has also offered safe haven to nearly three million Syrian refugees. It is for precisely these reasons why I find the events of May 16, 2017 so disturbing and why they are deserving of our strongest condemnation.

On May 16, 2017, protesters gathered outside the Turkish Ambassador's residence in Washington, D.C., to demonstrate opposition to the Turkish Government and President Trump's meeting with Turkish President Recep Tayyip Erdogan.

After hours of peaceful protest, pro-Erdogan supporters and Turkish security personnel brutally attacked the unarmed demonstrators. D.C. Police Chief Peter Newsham has confirmed that the attacks were unprovoked. As guests of the United States, Turkish government officials should demonstrate respect for American democratic institutions, like the rights of free speech and free assembly. Instead, they have demonstrated their intolerance for peaceful dissent in this and two previous incidents at the Brookings Institution in 2016 and the United Nations General Assembly in 2011.

My fellow Turkey Caucus co-chairs and I expressed our strongest regarding this assault on American democratic institutions, and called on the Turkish Government to issue an apology and to pledge to refrain from such incidents in the future. The House Foreign Affairs Committee also recently passed H. Res. 354 condemning the violence against peaceful protesters.

This shameful incident must be addressed immediately at the highest levels of government in a manner that engenders respect for democratic principles and promotes a constructive dialogue with our ally that respects democratic rights and norms in Turkey and here in Washington, D.C.